Understanding Business Process Re-engineering

in a week

John Macdonald

Headway · Hodder & Stoughton

Acknowledgements

The author and publishers would like to thank Business Intelligence Ltd for permission to include the material on pp. 67–9; and Texas Instruments for the diagram on p. 18.

British Library Cataloguing in Publication Data

A catalogue for this title is available from the British Library

ISBN 0 340 62103 6

First published 1995

Impression number	10	9	8	7	6	5	4	3	2	1
Year			1999	1998	1997	1996	1995			

Copyright © 1995 John Macdonald

All rights reserved. No part of this publication may be reproduced or transmitted in any form or by any means, electronic or mechanical, including photocopy, recording, or any information storage and retrieval system, without permission in writing from the publisher or under licence from the Copyright Licensing Agency Limited. Further details of such licences (for reprographic reproduction) may be obtained from the Copyright Licensing Agency Limited, of 90 Tottenham Court Road, London W1P 9HE.

Typeset by Multiplex Techniques Ltd, St Mary Cray, Kent. Printed in Great Britain for Hodder & Stoughton Educational, a division of Hodder Headline Plc, 338 Euston Road, London NW1 3BH by St Edmundsbury Press, Bury St Edmunds, Suffolk.

the Institute of Management

F O U N D A T I O N

The Institute of Management (IM) is at the forefront of management development and best management practice. The Institute embraces all levels of management from students to chief executives. It provides a unique portfolio of services for all managers, enabling them to develop skills and achieve management excellence.

For information on the benefits of membership, please contact:

Department HS
Institute of Management
Cottingham Road
Corby
Northants NN17 1TT

Tel: 0536 204222
Fax: 0536 201651

This series is commissioned by the Institute of Management Foundation.

The author can be contacted at:

John Macdonald Associates Ltd, 16 Woodcote Avenue, Wallington, Surrey SM6 0QY Tel. & Fax: 081-647 0160

C O N T E N T S

The competitive pressure to meet customer expectations is growing at an ever faster pace. The steady improvement of products and services is no longer sufficient to survive in the global market-place. The need is for a radical change in the way we all work. Business process re-engineering (BPR) can help organisations make that change.

The growth of BPR has been so rapid and experience so diverse that there is confusion as to what the term covers. In reality, BPR is the common-sense result of management making use of the new tools of information technology.

The aim of this book is to clear the confusion and provide an easy step-by-step guide to the understanding of the BPR process:

Sunday	–	Understanding the concept
Monday	–	Setting the direction
Tuesday	–	Selecting the people
Wednesday	–	Defining how to go about it
Thursday	–	Wiping the slate clean
Friday	–	Putting it into practice
Saturday	–	Continuous improvement

What is BPR?

BPR stands for 'Business Process Re-engineering'. The term is being used to cover three distinctly different management approaches to change. These are process improvement, process redesign and process re-engineering. Each is a valid approach to meet different circumstances. Today we will consider and define the differences between each.
The diagram on the opposite page graphically illustrates the range in scope between these approaches.

Process improvement

TQM, Kaizen and other continuous improvement initiatives put emphasis on process improvement. The organisation empowers the whole workforce to look for and implement improvements to all work processes. There is a tendency for the improvements to be small, confined within functional boundaries and focused on improving the existing system. Nevertheless, this approach has a powerful impact on the work culture of the organisation. Everyone in the company is involved and are oriented towards customers and processes. As we shall see later in the week, continuous improvement of processes will play an integral part in the success of the other approaches.

Process redesign

The majority of the organisations who use the term BPR are in reality engaged in process redesign. For most companies this approach represents radical change. However, it is not what Michael Hammer and James Champy meant by the word 'radical' in their famous book *Re-engineering the Corporation.*

Process redesign does concentrate on major processes which cross functional boundaries. It is generally strongly customer focused. It goes beyond improving the existing processes, and continually asks the question, 'should we be doing this at all?'

Differences between improvement, redesign and re-engineering

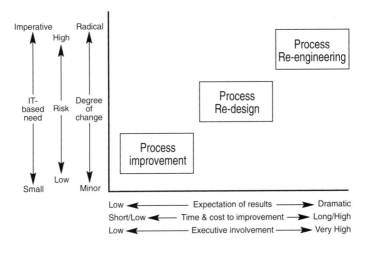

Process redesign is a natural evolution of TQM (see *Understanding Total Quality Management in a Week* in this series). It uses many of the traditional techniques of Organisation and Method (O & M) and Work Study. It differs from earlier approaches in its degree of customer focus and its use of the opportunities available from the development of information technology.

Business process re-engineering

Hammer has defined re-engineering as a 'fundamental rethink and radical redesign of business processes to achieve dramatic improvements in critical contemporary measures of performance, such as cost, quality, service and speed.'

The approach is based on the premise that continuous incremental improvement is not capable of meeting the challenge of the global market-place. To succeed, companies need major breakthroughs in performance and to leapfrog their competitors. BPR aims for dramatic improvements, not small steps to achieve slow and steady progress. Rather than 10 per cent improvements, BPR expects to cut product development cycles by 50 per cent, to cut order to delivery times from a month to one day and take 60 per cent to 80 per cent out of costs, while at the same time improving service levels. That is dramatic change.

Why did BPR evolve?

As with most conscious change, the spur is external to the organisation. The Japanese changed the perceptions of customers as to what they could and should expect. This spurred the quality revolution in the West, typified by such concepts as TQM. But for all the effort expended on quality initiatives, many companies felt that they were only playing 'catch up' on the world stage. They still needed major breakthroughs to create a sustained competitive advantage.

Throughout the eighties, the quality movement questioned traditional management behaviour and practices. The focus on customers and business processes stimulated

management thinking. At the same time, there was a growing comprehension of other factors impacting business.

New factors

The competitive revolution was accelerating and now impacted on public service organisations as well as industrial giants. New skill requirements on the workforce and the revolution of rising expectations made the division between 'thinkers and doers' unworkable. Above all, the technological revolution provided immense opportunities to challenge conventional wisdom.

Technology

Business, with some notable exceptions, has been slow to harness the revolution in information technology. Too often modern technology has been used just to speed up old-fashioned systems.

The revolution has been as much in software as in the visible hardware products. Relationable databases, communications technology and the power of the personal computer enable us to work in entirely new ways.

Information, including sophisticated design processes, can be shared on an instantaneous and continually updated basis. This means that key processes once designed to work sequentially in different functions can be started simultaneously anywhere. On a wider scale, it means that organisations can combine all the advantages of centralisation and decentralisation.

Realisation
Consideration of these factors should lead to a realisation of what is wrong with the traditional organisation of business. Most businesses are functionally organised in a way that obscures, and often totally hides, the key processes that drive performance and customer satisfaction.

Everyone involved in functional departments are focused on their own small part of the process rather than on the real objectives of the business, that is, on the creation and delivery of products and services that will delight customers.

Effective BPR

To use the elements of BPR to achieve an effective transformation from where we are to where we want to be is not easy. It requires a 'clean slate' or 'green field' approach to process redesign. The question that senior executives should be asking is this, 'If we are about to start this company with the knowledge we now have, how would it be organised?' The answers to that question will also determine the element of BPR most suited to the organisation.

Which elements?
The diagram on page 7 illustrated the radical change required and the dramatic results that can be achieved with full re-engineering. However, it also illustrated the high risks and the time and cost associated with the ultimate approach.

There is ample evidence that there is major risk and pain associated with re-engineering the total organisation. Some surveys have indicated that 50 per cent to 70 per cent of re-engineering efforts fail to achieve the goals originally set. These risks are compounded by the time it takes to accomplish the radical change.

A major division of the American giant AT & T has reported that within a two-year timescale, it had to accomplish the following in implementing re-engineering:

- Rewrite job descriptions for hundreds of people
- Devise new recognition and reward systems
- Modify all personnel policies
- Launch massive retraining
- Redesign the computer systems
- Change the financial reporting systems
- Develop new proposals and contracts
- Change the processes dealing with suppliers, manufacturing, shipping, installation and billing

All of that represents a great deal of upheaval and expense, and the business had to be carried on to the satisfaction of customers throughout the process of change.

TQM and BPR

Some proponents of BPR talk as if it had completely superseded TQM, which they brand as a failure. Nothing could be further from the truth. The two approaches are complementary rather than in opposition. Almost without exception the successful exponents of BPR have been and continue to be committed to the TQM process. Some would go as far as to say that you can't have one without the other!

The diagram on the opposite page illustrates the complementary nature of TQM and BPR. It also indicates the cultural framework which is essential to both processes. The framework is a main element of Tuesday's discussion.

One way of looking at the diagram on page 13 is to say that TQM provides the essential cultural framework to *enable* BPR. TQM puts a heavy emphasis on the need to change people's behaviour and attitudes. This change creates the environment for the successful implementation of BPR strategies.

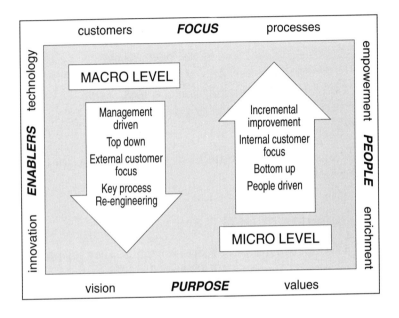

The principles of BPR

BPR has been described as discontinuous improvement rather than an element of continuous improvement. In other words a strategic decision to redesign how the business is managed.

The key principles of BPR which apply to both process redesign and process re-engineering can be summarised as follows:

- Customer driven
- Strategic in concept
- Concentrates on key business processes
- Cross functional
- Requires senior executive involvement
- Needs dedicated time of the 'best' people
- Will take time – it is not a quick fix
- Requires the communication of a clear vision
- Should target dramatic stretch goals

These principles will be examined in more depth as the week continues.

The benefits of BPR

The potential benefits of BPR are enormous. They are not easy to achieve, but there is substantial evidence that it can be effective. A financial services survey report on BPR provided the following example from re-engineering at an insurance company.

- Administration costs down by 40 per cent
- Staff turnover down by 58 per cent
- Claims settlements ratio down by 5 per cent
- New business applications up by 20 per cent
- Productivity increased by 100 per cent
- Claims handling time down from 28 days to four days
- Customer call-backs down 80 per cent

In the manufacturing arena equally dramatic results have been achieved:

- Order cycle time down from 33 days to three days
- Product development time reduced from 48 months to 10 months
- Productivity increased by 60 per cent

These claims are so great that it would be folly to ignore them. But be warned: there are risks.

Risks

Risks associated with BPR initiatives can be summarised as:

- The wrong processes are selected. They may be successfully redesigned, but if they are not core processes there is little impact on the business
- Senior executives are not directly sponsoring the process

- The team structure prevents innovative results
- Turf battles inhibit cross-functional implementation
- The resulting upheaval and costs far outweigh the results
- Process owners are not established

Over the next six days we shall examine a way to overcome these risks. We start on Monday by examining the direction our BPR initiative should take.

Summary

To sum up, BPR:

- Is a radical change in the way we work
- Aims to provide dramatic changes in performance
- Utilises the advances in information technology
- Is complementary to TQM
- Is customer driven
- Is process oriented

Where do we start?

On Sunday we highlighted the risks often encountered with BPR programs. Today, we start planning to eliminate those risks. We noted that often the wrong processes are selected for re-engineering. There are two principal reasons why this happens:

1   The executives are so focused on the expectation of benefits that they demand 'action this day'. In other words there is no time for reflection, assessment, analysis and planning.
2   Management have allowed their obsession with results, functions and hierarchies to obscure the real purpose of business processes.

Few executives are process oriented. Their business experience has focused their minds on tasks, jobs, functions, structure and people. This focus is also determined by the business concentration on results rather than on managing the processes to produce results (not a new management concept but an old Hindu philosophy called GITA). As a result executives do not understand that in their present organisation the existing business processes are designed for:

- Outdated technology
- Outdated management practices
- The business; not the customer

These attitudes create misconceptions about business process re-engineering. For example, BPR has little or nothing to do with 'downsizing' or 'restructuring.' These are reactions to recession and market conditions: 'We face a slack market so let's downsize.' Again, BPR is not designed to destroy business bureaucracies; they are actually the glue that hold organisations together. If the management focus is on processes they can be managed within and with the support of the bureaucracy.

BPR should lead management to ask some basic questions about their business strategy. These should include querying the current role of customers, owners, employees, suppliers and outside regulatory bodies in those strategies. So we must start the BPR journey by looking at our business in a new way. Texas Instruments, the American BPR pioneer, illustrate this with the diagram below:

Components of business process engineering

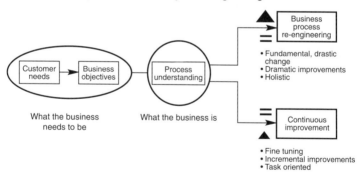

As we start our examination of the business it is worth noting some of the barriers that can inhibit radical change. They are:

- Traditional management behaviour
- Staff opposition based on fear of what change might bring
- Cost, overworked resources and time to achieve results
- Current company success
- Investment in current information technology (IT) and other systems
- Sheer size and/or geographic distribution of the business
- Fortress mentality
- Conventional wisdom

Executives, middle managers and other employees, in the main want to do a good job. There will be some personal agendas, but generally they are all united in that they want their company to be successful and respected. This poses the question, why then is success so difficult to achieve? Also, if there is this unity of purpose, why are so many organisations plagued with turf wars and adversarial relationships?

The answer is that, over this century, we have steadily made the practice of business so complicated and divisive that no individual can see the wood for their own favourite tree. The intriguing fact is that it has all been done on purpose in the name of enlightened management.

Adam Smith, Frederick Taylor and countless apostles demonstrated to businessmen that if they divided major processes into a host of small specialised processes they would achieve massive increases in productivity. They were proved right and the era of mass production began.

The process of specialisation continued and business became divided between the 'thinkers and doers'. Of course the doers had to be controlled and supervised because they could not think for themselves. So layers of functional middle management were gradually interspersed between the decision-makers and the real makers of product or deliverers of service. Business had developed the corporate dinosaur; its small head was so far away from its large feet that it took too long to change direction.

The pioneers of modern industry and commerce were right *at the time* and in the conditions in which they promulgated their ideas. But the conditions have changed. The progress of technology, education and customer and employee expectations have changed the business environment.

What the business needs to be

Business is quite simple; managers have made it appear complex. In functional terms only three positions really matter in the business process. They are the:

- Chief executive, who is responsible for determining the strategy of the business (resolving the inherent disputes between the other two) and organising the resources and support

- Marketing director, who is responsible for defining customer needs and wants and designing the products and services to satisfy the customers
- Production or operations director, who is responsible for developing the capability and then delivering the product or service to the customer

All other functions in the organisation are only there to support these processes. The clouding of these essential simple principles has led to the relative decline of Western industry. This can be illustrated by the following tendencies:

- The rise of the power of financial directors in the sixties led to an obsession with quarterly results and short-term financial thinking
- The rising influence of the personnel directors in the seventies (caused by government interference in industrial relations) sapped management's ability to manage
- The eighties have seen the growing influence of the public relations 'spin doctors' and the lawyers on business organisations. They are now seeking a seat at the strategic-business-making table

These and other tendencies have created habits of thought which are obscuring the true purpose of the key processes of business and public sector organisations. They only exist to satisfy customers. The diagram overleaf illustrates these arguments in process form.

The key processes of business

CUSTOMERS	CUSTOMERS	CUSTOMERS
DETERMINING CUSTOMER NEEDS AND WANTS	RESOLVING CONFLICTS	ORDER PROCESSING AND FULFILMENT
STRATEGIC PROCESS CUSTOMER FUNCTION MARKETING	STRATEGIC PROCESS STRATEGY FUNCTION CEO	STRATEGIC PROCESS DELIVERY FUNCTION MANUFACTURING OR OPERATIONS
DEVELOPING PRODUCTS OR SERVICES	FINANCE HR AND G&A LEGAL IT	DEVELOPING CAPABILITY

Communication ↔ Communication

OWNERS/SHAREHOLDERS

The simple diagram of key business processes above challenges a number of assumptions that are taken for granted in business organisation. For example:

- Selling is not a major process and is part of the delivery rather than the marketing process. Applied thought will indicate the dangers of relying on selling for market intelligence
- Order processing, billing and receivables are part of the delivery process. There is no business reason why these processes should be considered a separate administrative function or part of the financial function
- Research and product development are part of the customer-oriented marketing process

- Finance, human resources, general administration, legal, public relations and management information systems are not key business processes. They exist only to support the other processes. The sub-processes of these functions could easily be relocated in a *process-managed* organisation
- The chief executive's function is to resolve the natural issues that arise from the key processes and thus to determine the strategic direction of the organisation. A key part of this function is to provide support for the strategic decisions and to ensure that the owners agree to and support the strategy

As we continue to examine these issues we will realise that the new focus on the purpose of the organisation provides many reasons for radical change. One issue is clear. The purpose of business is to understand customer needs and then fulfil them.

Assessment

A companion volume *Understanding Total Quality Management in a Week* described the process of assessment within a company. The aim is to identify real need for change and the organisational barriers to change. The following guidelines are pertinent to the need for BPR:

- Senior management must recognise the need for change. BPR cannot succeed without committed management involvement
- Heavy current activity is not a valid reason to delay decisions: 'We cannot wait around for the storm to stop . . . we have got to work in the rain'
- Management and employees need to have a customer, process and teamwork culture
- The organisation must share a clear customer-oriented vision or purpose and supporting values

Customer driven

Business success and survival depends on strategies and processes directed to satisfying customers. This statement is a business truism which most executives readily accept. Unfortunately, too many believe that they do not need to talk to customers – they already know what the customers want!

Almost without exception, companies that actively seek customer views are surprised. Issues that the company believed dominated customer minds are found to be secondary. The strategy, and even the processes, have to be revised.

Standard customer or quality surveys rarely provide this level of powerful input. Unless the customer experience has been disastrous, the overall input of such surveys are generally good enough to create a feeling of comfort. A new competitor could dramatically change the customer's evaluation. Surveys also suffer from generalisation while business strategy is dependent on specifics.

Understanding customer needs and wants and *their* priorities within those categories requires a very specific and detailed approach. Identification of key customers for individual attention and organised focus groups of other customers should be a regular pattern of the business process.

The impact of technology

We are all aware of the pace of change in the technology that surrounds us, but few of us have had the time to absorb the difference that this technology will make on our personal and working lives.

In the 'white hot heat of the technological revolution' back in the sixties we were all promised that computers would take all the drudgery out of work and that we could all look forward to a life of comparative leisure. That didn't happen!

Then, in the seventies, businesses were promised that management information systems would revolutionise business decision-making. The man who believed and had his finger on the data processing button would command the market. That didn't happen!

In the eighties we were persuaded that the advent of the personal computer and the power of shared databases would empower the whole workforce. That didn't happen!

Based on all that experience, why should executives, middle managers and employees now believe that information technology is about to change their working lives and that they must adapt?

There was a germ of truth in all the predictions about computers; it is just taking longer to realise. This is common to the introduction of all technological advances. There is delay between proven concept and the ready availability of cost-effective, easy-to-use applications. An element in that delay is the time it takes potential users to comprehend fully what is available. That same pattern can be seen in the introduction of the internal combustion engine, the telephone, radio, television and the aeroplane.

Information technology has followed the traditional path. Just as early motor cars and railway carriages were designed to look like stage coaches, so early computers were used to duplicate the original handwritten processes. We are creatures of habit.

But the time comes when the habits are broken and the new technology is seen in its real guise and its potential is unleashed. That time has arrived for information technology. A critical mass of those in business now understand that they are not handling mere computing devices, but communication and information handling systems.

All the interlinked processes of organisations are primarily based on communication and information. The developed technology therefore provides the opportunity to reorganise, redesign or re-engineer those processes radically.

We therefore need a comprehension of the potential of information technology to make decisions about the validity of BPR. A valuable exercise used by some successful implementers was to start with 'technology visioning sessions' for senior management. The organisation may be lucky enough to have an individual capable of this level of communication within their own IT department. Otherwise these skills should be sought outside.

We shall return to the impact of technology on Thursday.

Key stakeholders

Earlier we emphasised that satisfying customer needs should be the prime driver of any BPR program. However, there are some other considerations which we ignore at our peril. Some will impose limitations on our ability to take a total 'green field' approach.

Owners
All organisations have owners. In service, institutional or local authority sectors, they may be in the form of an elected council of members. In the central government sector, they are seen as parliament or perhaps more directly as the Minister. In industry and commerce they are specific owners or, more usually, a large number of shareholders.

There is a perception that owners are only interested in short-term gains. Unfortunately, too many chief executives and/or chairmen appear to act in such a way as to make the perception self-prophesying.

If radical changes are to be made to the business, this needs to be presented to the owners to ensure their support over the long haul.

Employees
Employees have a major stake in change. They will certainly know that it is being planned and is to take place. They may have a number of reactions to the possibilities including the fear of job losses. Senior managers have some difficulty in communicating this issue to employees on the basis that it is like 'asking the turkeys to vote for Christmas'. The purpose of BPR is not 'downsizing', but it would be foolish in the extreme to pretend that a fundamental redesign of processes is not likely to result in job changes and potential job losses.

Whatever happens it is clear that jobs are likely to change dramatically. Failure to communicate a clear vision that recognises need from the employee's perspective will result in non-cooperation or, at its worst, substantial obstruction.

Suppliers

Organisations which have been involved in TQM initiatives will already realise that suppliers play an integral part in meeting customer requirements. Their involvement in the redesign of appropriate key business processes can provide the opportunity for them to become *real* business associates. Not only are they likely to redesign some of their processes to meet your needs, but this can also provide powerful new perspectives.

Outside bodies

We operate in a complicated world. There are all kinds of outside bodies which influence or even specifically regulate the processes of our organisation. For example, in the food processing and pharmaceutical industries, outside regulatory bodies define required health and safety standards. However, in many countries, they also define inspection and recording procedures which directly limit the use of new technology in process redesign. There is a need to change many of these regulations but in the meantime they do impose limitations on the 'clean slate' approach.

Opportunities for BPR

Clearly the business strategy and mission should be determinate in selecting the priority BPR projects. Within that context, processes may be selected on the basis of critical success factors or consideration of business significance.

Customer and internal assessments could highlight areas of customer concern, the degree of process failure and an assessment of ability to implement. There are also internal warning signs such as, long sequential activities, too much paper, too many controls or hands-offs, too much inventory or evidence of continual firefighting.

Finally it might be wise to keep in mind what surveys have shown to be the top five benefits that companies expect from their investment in BPR:

- Increased customer focus
- Improved profitability
- Improved quality
- Improved corporate flexibility
- Increased speed of service delivery

Summary

We have spent Monday considering the key issues we have
to clarify before embarking on a BPR project. These include:

- What the business needs to be
- What the business is
- The customer-driven objective of processes
- Benchmarking
- The importance of new technology
- Influence of outside bodies
- Strategy for BPR

Who's involved?

On Sunday and Monday we were introduced to the scope of BPR and its importance to the organisation. Today, we recognise that change, substantial or otherwise, can only be achieved by people. Eventually all the people will be involved in the change but at the outset the 'change masters' have to be selected.

Selection of the right people to drive each BPR project is crucial to the success of the initiative. Unless senior executives are fully involved, and some of the organisations 'best and brightest' people are dedicated full-time, there is little hope of dramatic results. BPR is not a quick fix, so these people will be committed for periods of from six to 18 months. This is 'bite the bullet' time right at the outset.

The number of people involved will differ depending upon the size of the company and the scope of the processes to be re-engineered. However, most BPR programs would require staffing for the following positions or teams:

- Champion
- Steering committee
- BPR Czar
- Outsiders
- Process design team
- Sub-process teams
- Process owner
- Implementation teams

We will spend the rest of Tuesday examining the staffing issues involved in each of these areas.

Champion

A senior executive must sponsor or *champion* a BPR project. There are too many cross-functional issues and strategic implications for the leadership of the project to be delegated.

Ideally the CEO will be the champion, though they may not have been the initiator. If there are several BPR projects, then the champions could be appointed from the senior operational directors.

There is a temptation to appoint the IT Director or the HR Director as champions of projects because of the impact of technology and people. This could be dangerous as they often have entrenched views in their own specialisation.

The champion must take a leading role in the BPR project. This is not a full-time post, but it does involve day-to-day leadership. The champion provides authority.

The role of the champion can be summarised:

- Establishes the breakthrough vision and goals
- Frees resources
- Empowers and holds employees accountable
- Resolves 'turf' issues
- Communicates and champions change

Steering committee

Most BPR projects cross major functional boundaries and by their nature will change or eliminate those boundaries. In many cases, BPR will also eliminate whole functions as currently organised. This is the tough part. There will be a natural tendency for many senior managers to defend their 'turf'.

Although the senior executives may understand the need for change, few understand how the process takes place. If they are to support the champion and the teams by 'walking the talk' they must keep track of what is happening.

A steering committee of senior executives (usually the management committee) will address these issues as they arise. This ensures the 'buy in' or ownership which will be vital during the implementation stage.

The role of the steering committee is to:

- Get issues on the table and resolve them
- Challenge assumptions
- Participate
- Form teams of the right people
- Remove obstacles or inhibitors to team success
- Ensure that appropriate metrics are used
- **Listen**

BPR Czar

Large organisations may have several BPR initiatives active at the same time. These will need to be coordinated and focused on the business strategy.

Also, as experience in BPR techniques develops within the organisation, it is important to ensure that this knowledge and skill base is not lost or dissipated. People with these skills can become future project leaders.

Both these issues can be addressed by establishing an internal consultant team of skilled BPR specialists. In BPR terminology the leader of this team is called the BPR Czar. The steering committee must be on guard that this team does not become another overhead empire. Another danger is that the Czar becomes too controlling and inhibits innovation.

At the beginning of the BPR journey this role is more often carried out by outside consultants who train staff in BPR techniques.

Outsiders

There are two crucial elements in the design and implementation of BPR that could lead to the use of outsiders:

- The availability or not of individuals with the skills and knowledge of BPR techniques
- The need to see the organisation and the business process from an entirely different perspective

External consultants can fulfil part of these roles. However, remember that not many consultants have substantial experience in this area. BPR is relatively new as an approach in its own right, so it is more important to look for experience and skills in specialists areas. These include process analysis and measurement, facilitation and project management, team-building and innovation, and perhaps above all, an attitude that will produce a flexible approach to fit the organisation.

We should not forget that the redesign of processes should be focused on serving the customer. Clearly, we have to assess customer needs and future wants. What better way to do this than to involve some customers in the design process? Their previous experience with your service is as important as their knowledge.

Suppliers are also an important part of many key processes. The leading exponents of TQM consider suppliers as business associates. The BPR teams could take a similar approach for appropriate processes.

Process design team

Selecting the members and establishing them as a cohesive team is the crucial task in BPR. We are not setting up a short-term task force to solve problems. We are re-engineering whole sectors of the business and the team may take a year to complete the design for the new business process. This is the moment when the champion and the senior executives start to demonstrate how serious they are about change.

The factors to bear in mind when selecting and establishing a process design team are:

- Composition
- Individual qualities
- Terms and future reward
- Outsiders
- Team building
- BPR training

Composition
The team should be composed of full-time members, each of whom should bring the requisite skills and attitudes to the project. In the author's experience, team dynamics suffer if the membership exceeds eight. If, from time to time, additional knowledge or skills are required they can be coopted for a short period. The sub-process teams are also available for support.

One danger must be avoided. At the outset there is a tendency to try and represent every area or function that is likely to be affected. This can be disastrous. Not only is the team too large, but members retain their turf loyalties.

The team must contain knowledge of the *key* processes involved, have a diversity of expertise, experience and disciplines. It is important to include an IT specialist and someone with knowledge of BPR techniques. In many cases, these are outsiders. BPR consultants may also provide assistance with member assessment as part of the selection process.

Individual qualities

The level of experience and knowledge required determines that the team members must be senior managers or specialists. The need for innovative and creative thought determines that the members should be selected from the 'best and brightest' talent available. Additionally, the team leader or captain must exhibit all those qualities together with the authority and credibility to get things done. They also need special training in team dynamics and facilitation.

Individuals with those qualities are usually already involved in key sectors of the business. If the organisation is not prepared to release them for an extended period, it would be wiser to forget all about BPR. This issue alone demonstrates the importance of the champion and the steering committee.

Terms and future reward

We have just discussed the calibre of team members required. The organisation must also see the situation from the individual's perspective. By definition, these individuals are already doing well and have strong career prospects in the organisation. Actually, they are going to help create a new organisation and their own next challenges. However, this is not clear at the beginning.

The champion must give careful consideration to this aspect before selecting the team. The role of team member should be treated as promotion and rewarded commensurately. The members should also be guaranteed a key role at the completion of their team duties.

Outsiders

The decision as to whether to include outside consultants to assist the process design team and the method of involving other outsiders should be taken before the team is established.

In operation the team leader should guard against the tendency for the outsider to 'go native'. This is a natural result of team dynamics, but it is not to the team's advantage. The worth of outsiders to the team's deliberations is based on their untrammelled perspective.

Team building

The establishment of the team in the sense of member selection can lead to the temptation to leap into immediate action. The leader must have the patience to concentrate members' attention on learning first how to work as a team.

A team-building course or workshop is an essential element in the BPR process. If this capability does not exist in the organisation, there are many competent consultants in this discipline.

As part of the team-building exercise the leader should give consideration to the team's working space. To break the private turf patterns, team members should not continue to work from their existing offices.

BPR training
Team members will also need training in the techniques used in BPR. Many have been derived from O & M and TQM practices and therefore some members may be familiar with them. The essential techniques are process mapping, simulation, statistical and other measurement methods, and the team decision techniques.

As a company's experience grows, internal consultants in the Czar's domain will be able to provide this expertise. Otherwise all are readily available outside.

The role of the process design team is to:

- Map the existing processes involved
- Challenge all assumptions
- Accept no boundaries
- Remain customer focused
- Find breakpoints to support the strategy
- Design the new process
- Establish pilot proving plans
- Define the measurement criteria

- Recommend and present implementation plans to the champion and steering committee
- Recognise continually the need for communication with all involved

Sub-process teams

In large organisations functional and geographic dispersion have complicated business processes and obscured the purpose of the business. Even without these complications each key process is subdivided into a host of sub- or small scope processes. It is vital that the process design team is not so drowned in detail that it cannot find the breakpoint strategy.

Nevertheless, the implications of the design team's recommendations on the small processes have to be considered before the final implementation plans are completed.

Sub-process teams should be established to map the small scope processes. This equips them to challenge the assumptions of the process design team. Some of those challenges may lack the overall perspective, but equally, some may highlight a potential flaw in the design team's plans.

Sub-process teams do not require full-time members and are usually composed of individuals working in the specific sub-processes.

Process owner

Once the process design team's recommendations have been accepted by the champion and the steering committee, the implementation phase can begin. The process design team can now be recognised and disbanded.

The first step in implementation is for the steering committee to appoint a *process owner*. This individual will be responsible for the *actual re-engineering* and accountable for the new process goals. This will include both the pilot and full implementation phases (these areas will be developed on Friday).

The process owner will be a senior line manager and should normally be selected from the members of the process design team.

The process owner is a major full-time post which is intended to have a dramatic impact on business performance. It will also play a major part in the cultural transformation from a functional to a process-based organisation.

The role of the process owner is to:

- Ensure that the plans are fully implemented
- Obtain and organise the necessary resources
- Select the implementation team
- Overcome resistance from incumbents and the bureaucracy
- Manage the new process
- Ensure that the initial gains are maintained and continuously improved (we will develop this area on Saturday)

Implementation teams

The implementation teams are effectively the supervisors and managers of the newly designed process. They will be selected from those displaced in the old processes and/or members of the process design team and the sub-process teams.

As we will see later, the implementation phase is substantial, and may well take some 18 months from the acceptance of the process design team's recommendations.

These teams will also include some specialists, particularly in the IT areas, who may be assisting with the development of new systems to support the implementation. Some of these specialists are likely to form part of the BPR Czar's internal consultant teams.

People and culture

The term 'business process re-engineering' sounds so mechanistic that it is very easy to ignore the people and cultural aspects of BPR. The macro/micro level diagram on page 13 was enclosed by a framework designed to hold the whole improvement process together. As today we are discussing the involvement of people in the process, it is an appropriate place to revisit that sector of the framework.

In some quarters, BPR has been greeted as a new realism which concentrates on business measurables. In that context TQM is derided as *mere* culture change and dismissed as a waste of money and effort. Yet the companies that have been able to demonstrate dramatic improvements in business performance with BPR all emphasise the cultural element. Motorola, Xerox, Texas Instruments, Wal-Mart, AT & T and the British Prudential Assurance Company are all on record as saying that the TQM or continuous improvement movement is an essential element of a successful BPR strategy.

TQM demands a customer and process focus. It calls for the establishment of a clear vision and the sharing of purpose and values with all employees. TQM also highlights the change in management behaviour required to empower employees to realise their potential. This is at the root of enabling employees to enrich their working lives; to find joy in work.

BPR has harnessed the enablers of technology and the release of the innovative potential of people to achieve leapfrogging or breakpoint scales of change. BPR is centred in the TQM movement and requires its cultural framework for ultimate success. Both are about breaking out of the functional 'turf' thinking to process thinking.

Summary

We have spent Tuesday considering the involvement of people in the BPR process. Our discussion covered the following key areas:

- The importance of senior management involvement
- The assistance we can get from people outside the organisation
- The selection of the 'brightest and best'
- The need to motivate and reward
- The handover from design to implementation
- The key role of the process owner, Czar and champion
- The synergy between BPR and TQM

Methodology

On Tuesday, we discussed the people involved and the establishment of the 'change masters' and teams. We now need to create a framework and discipline for these people to work within.

A BPR project on a key business process can last as long as two years or more, from selection to the completion of measured feedback and assessment.

From a management point of view we have to break this long period into a number of phases. There are four phases as follows:

- Phase one – Preparation
- Phase two – Innovation
- Phase three – Implementation
- Phase four – Assessment

Each of the phases have a number of elements or stages. Today we will spend our time on Phase One – Preparation. The other phases will be developed over the next three days.

Phase one – Preparation

Phase one can itself be divided into a number of stages. These stages are discrete though not necessarily sequential. They are as follows:

1   Defining objectives

2   Educating the team

3   Mapping the overall process model

4   Mapping the sub-processes

5   Defining customer needs

6   Defining business strategic needs

7   Envisaging breakthroughs

8   Steering committee approval

9   Champion defines design objectives

We will spend the rest of today considering these stages.

Defining objectives

The senior management of the organisation have to define the strategic objectives of the business. When married to the principles and values of the company, they create a vision, but in this world of change, objectives and visions do not remain static.

The need for BPR often stems from a management review of the strategic objectives. This review can stem from a number of driving forces. Recession and competitive pressure are prime examples. Privatisation for British Telecom or deregulation for the financial services industry also helped drive BPR programs.

As the result of management sessions, a new business strategy is developed. The decision is also taken to redesign the key processes of the organisation in line with the business strategy or 'the business we want to be'. The champion and the steering committee will define the BPR objectives and establish the BPR team.

The team leader or captain (possibly assisted by an outside consultant) has the task of building a team. Primarily the leader has to ensure that the objectives are not only understood but that the team takes collective ownership of them. They also have to agree their method of working and the key milestones.

Taking ownership of the objectives is not simple, as they are likely to be of a nature well outside the experience of team members. Typical radical BPR objectives are:

- Reduce operating expenditure by 60 per cent while improving the service to customers
- Reduce the time to produce and deliver an insurance policy for life cover from 21 days to three days

Unless the first reaction to the objectives is 'you must be joking' or similar, they are probably not radical or dramatic enough. Real ownership of these stretch goals comes about when the team fully comprehends the freedom and level of empowerment they have been given. We shall develop this aspect of BPR on Thursday.

The team has been empowered to 'slay sacred cows' or ignore the traditional fortresses of hierarchy. This new-found freedom has to be tempered with clear agreement on the methods and directions in which the team will work. The discipline should include an early schedule of milestones for project development.

This preliminary stage has established for the team *why* they are here; now they have to learn more about *how* it is going to be done.

Educating the team

The first priority of the team leader is 'team building'. This is not as easy as it may sound. The members have been selected from the 'brightest and best' and may also include outsiders. As individuals, they are likely to be strong personalities, be accustomed to taking the lead and may also have their own agendas. This could prove a volatile cocktail.

Investment in a team-building workshop at this stage will prove to be money and time well spent in the months ahead. Practice with the techniques of transactional analysis and the development of synergy provides a solid base for the team. The process builds respect for the individuals' disparate skills and a sense of trust in each other. A confident team can work in a relaxed atmosphere, but at the same time exhibit sustained concentration and hard work. This is more likely to bring about 'breakthrough' thinking.

To equip the team to take the 'helicopter' view of the company new skills have to be developed and knowledge acquired in the following areas:

- Process mapping (similar to O & M techniques)
- Opportunities provided by technology development (this is a broad appreciation for most of the team, which may already have individuals with in-depth expertise)
- Current market-place, competitors and relevant legislation or other external influences
- Customer perspectives. This could include visits to key customers
- Company's long-term business and product strategies

This preliminary education and training may be provided by internal or external sources. In essence it is a mixture of briefing sessions and specific courses. This whole area is an important element of the team leader's work and he or she may need some ad hoc resources to help with organisation.

The preparatory period takes patience, but it is invaluable. There is a natural tendency to want to get started quickly on the objectives of the project. As Abraham Lincoln said, 'If I had four days to cut down a tree, I would spend three days sharpening the axe.' Perhaps extreme, but we are honing specific skills and knowledge and, above all, building teamwork.

Mapping the overall process model

We started by developing an understanding of 'what the organisation wants to be' in terms of strategic goals to meet customer and business needs. Before shaping the process to meet those goals we must also comprehend the 'business as it is'. At this stage, it is important that we concentrate on the big picture, rather than become immersed in detail. This is sometimes called taking the 'helicopter view'.

The key process flow diagram on page 22 was nearer to a 'satellite view' of business. It was aimed at illustrating the basic simplicity of business and reflecting on some relationships between functions and processes. Our diagram illustrated three strategic processes and one organisation-wide set of supporting processes. The strategic processes were called 'customer', 'strategy' and 'delivery'. The supporting services include what we more often consider as functions such as finance, legal, personnel and public relations. In one sense, this diagram establishes a corporate value system.

These strategic processes can be broken down into a number of key, but still very large, processes. In turn, these key processes themselves break down into a multiplicity of sub-processes. It would be wrong to consider them as minor because the chain of processes is only as strong as its weakest link. Nevertheless, it does become a matter of substantial detail and could obscure the bigger picture.

A quick look at one of the strategic processes in the diagram, namely 'delivery', shows the breakdown into key and sub-processes. The key processes include: developing manufacturing and delivery capability, product manufacture, order processing and fulfilment. The latter process breaks down into distribution, delivery, sales order processing, payments, billing and receivables.

In the past we have treated all these linked processes as though they were a pack of playing cards. The cards, or individual processes, were dealt out to departments as functional hands. From then on, in the game of business, they were played as separate hands rather than a complete pack. To continue the analogy we now have to reorganise the cards into their main suits.

To be more prosaic, the diagram below breaks down one strategic process of an insurance company, 'renewal policy issuance', into its major processes. This is still an overview, as we shall see later, but it does help us understand what is happening. This simple mapping across the business provides an overall process model.

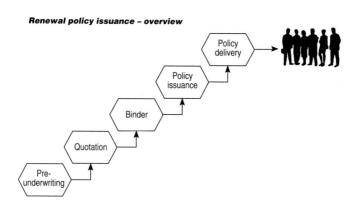

Renewal policy issuance – overview

Mapping the sub-processes

The strategic process 'renewal policy issuance' in the last diagram showed the breakdown into major processes. Before the whole redesign process can take place this again will have to be broken down into sub-processes.

Selecting one of the simpler major processes in the diagram, that of 'Binder' the next two diagrams show how this process breaks down. The dotted lines indicate the flow of the process through departments.

Strategic and key process mapping is a substantial task in a large organisation. Sub-process mapping is infinitely more detailed as our diagrams show. It also requires people with working knowledge of the processes.

As each stage of the strategic and key process review is completed, the sub-process teams can be established. Key processes can be much more complex than our insurance company example. Some companies have formed 30–40 sub-process teams involving a large number of people.

Some of the elements of team building noted earlier would be useful at this stage, though not so critical. These are not full-time teams and they will only be together for limited periods. However, they will need guidance on mapping techniques.

For large organisations, this is a major step requiring coordination and communication. This underlines the need for the BPR Czar in a big company. A substantial spread of sub-process teams creates issues of sponsorship, but this function is generally exercised by the process design team leader.

"As is" binder process flow – pg 1

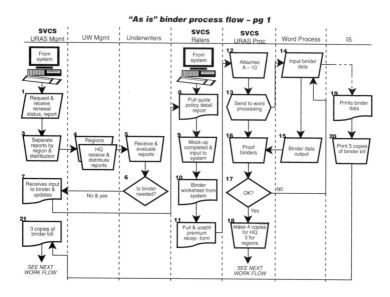

"As is" binder process flow – pg 2

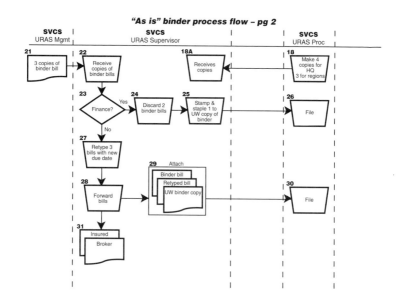

It should be emphasised that these reviews of 'how the business is' contain a great deal more information than flow charts. The reports and data included in this task can be summarised as:

- Process descriptions
- Flow charts
- Technology characteristics
- Customer satisfaction weighting
- Activity descriptions
- Functional characteristics
- Performance measures
- Revenue weighting

Defining customer needs

Our process design team has already looked at strategy from a customer perspective. This may well have included some key customer visits. This activity now has to be expanded so that a detailed report on customer needs can be assembled.

During the mapping, activity processes were weighted as to their influence on the customer. This provides us with powerful information on the areas in which clarification of customer need can be sought. Bland questionnaires about customer satisfaction will normally receive a 'good' answer unless something catastrophic has happened recently. This level of customer feedback is useless to those aiming for 'breakthroughs' in customer service.

The questioning of customers has to be carefully planned and directed. The questions must be focused on eliciting customer perception of performance in meeting current needs and their view of their future needs. Perhaps more important *each* of their present and future needs must be rated as to its importance to *their* business. Many companies have been deluded by customer surveys which indicated a very high proportion of 'ticks' against a particular need. Quantity ruled but in truth they were a minor need for most individual customers. Substantial effort was diverted to satisfy a minor need while each major individual need may have been relatively ignored.

There are many techniques for eliciting customer need. Choice for individual organisations will depend on the nature of their business or service. The range includes:

- Ongoing communication with a strong 'user' group
- Specialist external consultants
- Questionnaires/surveys
- Focus groups of selected customers
- 'Independent' surveys seeking supplier ranking
- Phone interviews

Defining business strategic needs

The oft-used terms 'the customer is king' and 'driven by customer need' have become hackneyed in quality initiatives. They are in danger of losing their essential meaning. Meeting the need of *every possible* customer is patently absurd. It that's not so then Volkswagen and Rolls Royce are in the same market. Describing their market as 'providing motor cars' is not sufficiently precise as a market definition and has obvious dangers as a business strategy.

For business, the strategic decision is *which* customers are kings. Many factors will determine that decision. These will include resources, core competencies, characteristics of the market, perceived changes in the market-place and other external factors. For example, the period of deregulation in financial services made dramatic changes in market conditions. All sectors of the industry were involved in totally redefining their business strategies. Some made massive mistakes while others prospered.

The successful strategies are always those that can match business needs and characteristics with customer needs. Our team must now concentrate on first defining the business needs and then meshing them with their previous work on customer needs.

Envisaging breakthroughs

It is now time for the team to bring together all the strands of the preparation stage ready for the innovation and design stage.

A brainstorming or 'visioning' workshop for the design team, often with outside consultant help, is a key milestone activity.

The objective of the workshop is to establish the critical success factors and guiding vision statements. The whole activity will unify the design team around the parameters for the whole BPR program. The 'breakthrough' theme, which lies at the heart of BPR, will be developed on Thursday.

Steering committee approval

The interim results and views of the design team should now be presented to the steering committee. This helps to ensure senior management awareness and continued support for the programme.

The presentation should include the strategic and customer needs analysis, the envisioned future design and the design and implementation issues. The success factors and the milestones are key; this is a management approval exercise rather than an information presentation.

This is also one of the last opportunities to resolve any resource, communication or power barriers before real change is launched.

Champion defines design objectives

The concluding act for Wednesday lies with the BPR Champion. The views and decisions of the steering committee must now be translated into clear objectives for the design team.

These objectives will drive the next stage of innovation and design which is the subject for Thursday.

Summary

We have spent Wednesday preparing for the redesign of our organisation. Our discussion covered the following subjects:

- The overall methodology for BPR
- Educating and preparing the team
- Mapping the key and sub-processes
- Defining customer needs
- Clarifying strategic objectives
- Achieving management approval for the next stage

Innovation

On Wednesday, we discussed the four phases of a BPR
project and concentrated on Phase one – Preparation. Today
we will look at the next phase.

Phase two – Innovation and design

Phase two involves discussion of a number of issues and
stages as follows:

- Visioning
- Encouraging innovation
- The role of information technology
- Realism
- Future design
- Benefit analysis
- Organisational preparation for change
- Implementation planning

Visioning

On Wednesday, the BPR design team developed guiding vision statements for the BPR program. These statements should be dominated by the concept of a customer-driven organisation. The vision should represent an organisation changing from one:

- Organised around traditional management functions to one based on customer oriented processes
- In which products and support services determine strategy to one in which customer needs determine products and services
- Which uses information for internal control to one whose IT services are designed to empower employees to serve customers
- Which exhibits many faces to the customer to one which provides one point of contact and an unified face to the customer
- In which employees are internally or 'boss' focused to one in which all are clearly focused on the customer

These vision statements should be used by the team captain to encourage innovation. They will assist the team to break the barrier of the 'deadly clean sheet'.

Encouraging innovation

Teams can be constrained by traditional boundaries to thought. Experience leads many people to think within functional boxes. For example, most business people mistakenly consider that the billing and collection processes must be part of the finance function. In the BPR process, the team has to think 'outside the boxes' and forget the boundaries.

The purpose of innovation is to find 'breakthrough' solutions to our process issues. Teams must be given a clear lead and *permission* to:

- Question authority
- Question the limits of existing systems or technology
- Identify false assumptions
- Ask why

The innovative element to design can start with some simple questions which aim to find opportunities for change in the existing processes. Careful review of the 'as is' process maps would find possibilities if:

- A process goes back to a person or department where it was before
- A process reaches a control or approval point
- Sequential functions are split between multiple employees
- A process is manual but could be automated
- There are points in the process where work is waiting to be done

- An inappropriate level of authority or skill of staff is performing a function
- Work is slowed down by crossing functional or departmental boundaries
- A process is duplicated

This level of questioning may not produce the fundamental breakthroughs, but as an initial step, it is highly likely to break traditional thinking.

Driving creativity

The last exercise concentrated minds on process issues. Now the team has to use all the knowledge and goals established in the preparation phase to design new processes. The preparatory stage provided the team with substantial knowledge of:

- Customer hierarchy of needs and wants
- Strategic intent of the organisation
- Benchmarking data from competitors and/or high achievers
- Guideline vision statements and goals

Each of these drivers can be combined with process knowledge in a series of brainstorming sessions to determine the higher level of the new process designs.

The team leader must manage the brainstorming sessions and keep the following in mind:

- Establish tight deadlines. The information and analysis required has already been developed
- Don't limit thinking to feasible options. Challenge the answers from customer viewpoints. Be radical
- Never be constrained by previous 'best' performance figures. You are looking for major breakthroughs
- Don't be constrained by the 'best' competitor's performance figures. You are aiming to leapfrog the competition
- Don't be constrained by current organisational politics or conjectures about future political power bases. Your proposals may so change the environment that all those considerations become irrelevant

Role of information technology

Several times this week we have stressed the importance of technology in providing the opportunity for radical change.

None of this should be taken to mean that the current IT department must play a leading part in the BPR process.

Too many organisations invest in expensive upgrade or redesign of IT systems which merely duplicate or slightly improve existing processes. The IT department must be held back until their services are needed. Logically, they cannot design systems until the processes they support have been redesigned or re-engineered.

From the outset we have stressed the importance of IT as an enabler in the re-engineering of business processes. But if the IT department is to play its full role in process re-engineering, it needs to adopt a radically different approach towards its contribution to the organisation. Business Intelligence Ltd in 1992, produced one of the best reports on the progress of business re-engineering. (*Business Re-engineering: the use of process redesign and IT to transform corporate performance*, Business Intelligence, 1992.) This report noted 10 lessons for the IT function which are paraphrased below:

Share the vision: it is no longer enough for IT to perceive its function as converting business specifications into workable systems. IT professionals need to understand the business strategies of the organisation as a whole. Only then will they be able to utilise their technical skills to move the corporation towards its vision.

Envision the possible: senior IT executives should prepare regular briefings for other executives on how IT could help shape the business vision.

Provide the infrastructure: organisations are going to need sophisticated systems and a communications infrastructure to enable new applications. IT should take the lead in developing flexible and robust infrastructures to meet future challenges. This includes laying down 'ground rules' about standards, operating systems, data references, screen layouts and other issues.

Provide a strategy for system building: as the number of process re-engineering projects increases in an organisation, the IT function needs to develop methodologies and system development skills appropriate to BPR. IT professionals are able to access a growing range of tools such as relational database management systems, fourth-generation languages, and graphical user interfaces to assist the process.

Provide information systems skills as a generic resource for BPR: IT people have many of the skills that are needed in BPR projects. They can bring more to the party than pure IT knowledge. The IT function should maintain a close supportive relationship with the BPR Czar.

Add value to the process: increasingly, IT will be judged by its ability to add value to a process rather than its ability to automate procedures. The IT function must also develop the skill to think 'outside the box'.

Ensure timely delivery: IT departments have a poor reputation for on-time delivery of systems. This is partly due to the difficulty they have communicating with users, but some of the delay is due to their 'technology' stance. Users would rather have 80 per cent of what they want on time, rather than 100 per cent two years late and obsolete.

Help users to understand the technology: emphasis has been placed on the importance of the need for executives and BPR team members to envision technology. An essential element of the whole change process is to ensure that managers and people have a growing comprehension of the contribution technology can make to helping them. The IT function in the future must pay as much attention to communication and training as to the design of systems. It should be viewed as part of the IT department's responsibility that there are no technological barriers to non-technological people using the power of technology.

Help the BPR team own the IT: the IT element of organisations has increasingly exhibited the fortress mentality highlighted by TQM. IT is now so intimately woven into a re-engineered process, that the 'we are different' approach cannot be tolerated. The IT function must help users to 'own' the IT part of the process.

Be pro-active: the IT department should not wait for requests or complaints from users before considering change. It must always be in a position to suggest how IT can be used to make an enhanced contribution to a process. It should be alive and receptive to user requests for changes and amendments. IT has a key role to play in continuous improvement.

A survey report on the use of BPR asked the question 'do you expect technology to be critical to the success of BPR and if so which technologies would you identify?' The following is a list of technologies cited with those marked * most often named:

Client/service architecture*	Integration with existing databases
Document image processing*	Cooperative processing
New database technologies	Executive information systems
Workgroup applications	Behavioural scoring
Process-based systems	Expert systems
Decision-support systems	Local area networks
Knowledge-based systems	Satellite
Electronic data interchange	Card reading devices
Facsimile	Common graphical user interfaces
Bar coding	
Personal computers	Laptops
Workflow management*	

Realism

Each new management technique or development will sooner or later be dismissed as 'last year's fad'. Usually this is in reality a rejection of the over-zealous protagonists who are proclaiming the 'only true way'. But the art of science or management is not so easily compartmentalised. Most of the new concepts have something to offer; most provoke thought and positive action.

The fault is in the temptation to see each idea as a panacea for business. In truth, each new approach needs to be subjected to some healthy scepticism. In the author's view, it is time to inject an element of realism into the BPR movement.

Very few companies have the ability to manage the radical level of change demanded by the BPR idealists. Castigating their management as business dinosaurs due for extinction is of little help. Some managements see the risks of the over-radical route as so extreme as to lead to almost immediate extinction. These organisations need to see their operations from a different perspective, i.e., a customer- and process-oriented perspective which leads to a continuous effort of substantial change: radical, in their terms, but still manageable.

Future design

The preparatory work is now complete. The process design team is now in a position to begin redesigning or re-engineering the selected high priority process (or processes).

To illustrate the redesign phase we can return to the simple 'binder process flow' we examined in the diagrams on pages 54 and 56 on Wednesday. These diagrams graphically represented the 'as is' flow of that process. The diagrams on page 73 show the same process after redesign. The interim stage in the top diagram shows the elimination of many sub-processes. This in turn allows the compaction of the ultimate process shown in the bottom diagram.

A process moving through several functions with all the attendant delays and opportunities for error has been dramatically reduced. In fact functionality is almost irrelevant and the process can now be viewed as a single team operation.

This of course is a very simple process in the context of overall company strategic redesign. However, it does serve to illustrate some of the principles of redesign.

We must also understand that this is only a graphical representation of what is involved in redesign. The total work of redesign will include the following:

- Development of new IT systems
- Redefinition of job descriptions
- Multiskill education and training
- Development of new documentation
- Development of new procedures
- Communication to those involved in other processes
- New purchasing policies and contracts

The final stages of the innovation phase are not distinct or sequential. Benefit analysis, planning for change and implementation are integral parts of preparation, visioning and redesign.

These stages have been highlighted separately to emphasise that they are key responsibilities of the steering committee rather than the process design team.

Interim binder process flow

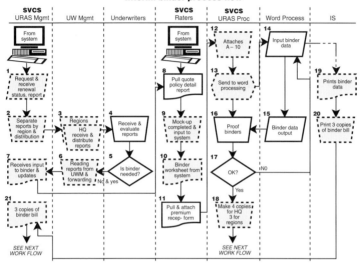

Ultimate binder process flow

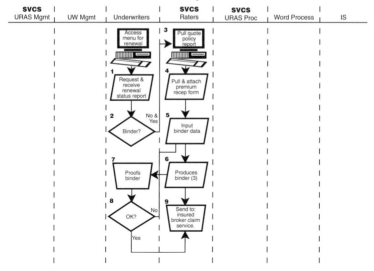

Benefit analysis

A contributory factor in the failure of many quality or improvement initiatives has been the lack of real business measurables. The process of change cannot be managed if performance indicators are not included in the evaluation procedures we will discuss on Saturday. This is the time to put a stake in the ground.

The benefit analysis should include the costs to implement, the expected financial savings, the impact on customers, and a definition of the risks envisioned in accomplishing the vision. These performance indicators are not 'wish list' statements but clear and measurable criteria.

Organisational preparation for change

The early preparatory stages of BPR should make it clear that that re-engineering of processes will have a profound effect on the structure and procedures of the organisation.

The key areas of change which will require applied thought *outside* the process redesign are:

- Restructuring the basic organisation and reporting patterns
- Personnel policies including the whole payment and reward structure
- Multiskill, leadership, teamwork and empowerment education and training
- Redeployment planning

The accomplishment of these activities requires planning and the establishment of directed task forces reporting to the steering committee.

Implementation planning

The redesign of processes is one thing, the implementation of the new approach is another. There are many traps and opportunities for compromise in the implementation phase. We will examine these issues in detail on Friday, but there is a need to define clearly the implementation at the design stage.

Summary

We have spent Thursday examining the issues involved in Phase two – Innovation. These have included:

- Thinking 'outside the box'
- Driving the process by customer strategies
- The important of technology
- Role of the IT function
- Holding on to realism
- Design issues
- Bringing it all together

Implementation

All the issues that we have considered during this week have really only been the preparation for Phase three – Implementation. Theory and planning are over; now we have to make it happen.

From Sunday, we have been looking for radical change to produce dramatic results. Experience and everything that we learnt should have served as a warning that implementation is difficult. Even successful BPR implementation has proved complex and painful for many of the people involved.

Implementation of a major process, from pilot to final acceptance, can take as long as two years. Over that time, the implementation team will encounter many frustrations. IT has dominated the design phase but it will have only a peripheral influence on the success or failure of implementation. The pervading issues will centre around people and the organisational culture.

The most difficult changes, for most organisations, are developing new skills and refocusing the attitudes of middle and supervisory management. To ensure that these impediments are overcome, Phase three must be focused on the following areas:

- Implementation plan
- Pilot proving
- Goals and objectives

- Rational metrics
- People
- Teamwork
- Education and training
- Communication

Pilot proving

Radical change is accompanied by substantial risk. In BPR, the risks are heightened by the length of time needed to complete implementation and to produce measurable results. These risks can be compounded by the natural management pressures 'to get on with it'. This is another moment for 'axe sharpening'. The new design has to be proven step by step before the whole organisation can operate in the changed mode.

The design team will have developed models of the new operations in action. For the steering committee and for their own benefit, the team will have used a variety of simulation techniques to prove the effectiveness of the new approach. However, simulation can never reproduce live working. There are too many factors outside the control of the process owners to simulate wholly a process in action. Not least are the factors of human behaviour of both employees and customers.

For these reasons the newly designed process should first be implemented in pilot mode. The nature of the pilot will clearly depend on the process, the type and size of the business, and the market. It is important that pilot operation is of sufficient scope to ensure that the process is fully proven. The scope must include volume processing and the full use of the various interfaces involved in the process. The pilot should continue for a period that allows measurement against all the criteria established to prove the process. Evaluation of the pilot will determine the pace of full implementation.

Goals and objectives

At the completion of the design stage the goals and objectives for the redesigned process must be agreed with the process sponsor and the steering committee. Before implementation, clearly defined goals must be communicated to all process participants.

For a major process, there could be a substantial number of goals and objectives. At the highest level, the overall goals would indicate the prime objective of the process. For example, to reduce the time taken to issue an insurance policy from 21 to three days. Still, at the high level, goals could be established to measure the number of people involved and the operational cost of the process. The overall process is likely to be subdivided into a number of sub-processes. Each element will have its own goals to enable the process to be measured by the participants in operation. If all the sub-goals are being met then it is highly likely that the overall goal will be met.

Seen in their entirety, the goals and objectives are the input and output requirements of every element of the re-engineered process. Some of those requirements will be selected for continuous measurement, and the selection will be varied from time to time. Every participant in the process has the right to know what is expected of them. In turn, they are empowered to measure those elements of requirements which they consider crucial to the continuous success of their work. The use of high level measures alone might provide data which is too late to identify disturbing trends. It can also hide a lot of variation at the lower level.

Measurement is the outward sign of inward grace or, to put it in another way, the real proof of a performing process. The continuous measurement of the sub-elements in the process enables the process owner and the participants to *manage the process*, not merely the results of the process.

Clearly, the development of goals and objectives on this scale will not be accomplished as some afterthought to the design process. The design team must see that as the new processes are designed, metrics for the performance of the process are designated. In some companies a specific individual on the team has taken the responsibility to ensure that this happens; in one case he was known as 'the measurement man'.

Rational metrics

When developing the measures for the newly designed process, the design team should bear in mind the following principles. Effective metrics should be:

- Process rather than function oriented
- Focused on the process customer requirements – either internal or external
- Relevant to the objectives of the process owner
- Easily understood by process participants
- Easy to collect or measure
- Cost effective in relation to their usefulness
- Focused on performance
- Displayed and communicated to appropriate people

Above all the process owner and the participants must not forget the purpose of measurement. Measurement provides continuous verification that the process is performing against the goals.

Failure to establish and then maintain measurement at all levels of the process has been the key factor in the disappointing performance of both TQM and BPR initiatives in many organisations.

People

Any organisation-wide initiative which involves change in the way of working is likely to lead to fear and uncertainty among employees. The BPR design team might describe their work as the transformation of existing processes, practices and procedures. The people effected may view 'transformation' as upheaval and chaos. At the very least, the nature of their jobs will change, and for many, their employment may be on the line.

These cultural and personnel issues cannot be ignored. The implications of BPR on personnel policies and people management are often only recognised in a reactive mode in the midst of the change implementation. This can be disastrous as the whole concept of radical change becomes clouded with conflict and compromise.

The redesign of processes and work methods is not a mechanistic exercise. People work in processes, and process performance depends on people. Therefore intelligent re-engineering will include the people issues as fundamental elements of the design process. Successful implementation demands that these factors have been resolved at design stage and form part of the pilot-proving criteria.

The leading researchers, Business Intelligence Ltd, have identified the five significant change management problems met by organisations in implementing BPR. They are:

- Changing the roles and responsibilities of existing staff to meet process requirements
- Anticipating and assessing the full scale of change entailed in re-engineering
- Retraining and re-skilling staff to manage and run the redesigned process
- Rewarding and motivating staff to achieve new goals
- Implementing new processes while keeping the business running

Each of these problems contain, or are dominated by, a people dimension. The implementation of BPR will involve all of the elements of human resource management. For many organisations, the personnel answers will take them into new territory such as gradeless management structures, multi-disciplinary teams and team-oriented compensation.

Personnel policy group
The people dimension is of such importance to the success of BPR that it must have a high-level focus. A recommended approach is for the sponsor to form a personnel policy group at the same time as the process design teams are established. This group should report to the steering committee.

Personnel specialists will be members, but the group is not an extension of the Personnel or HR Department. The group's purpose is to bring the process attitude of 'no sacred cows' to personnel policies of the organisation. Process design team leaders will be members of the group so that all are aware of the results of the visioning work on processes.

The result of the group's work should be the development of personnel policies and procedures that will support the smooth working of the re-engineered organisation. At the same time, they should pay particular attention to the problems of transition which may include redundancies. Education and training are key elements but training long-term employees for new skills raises a number of motivational issues which must be addressed.

It is very easy for the leaders of the BPR process to lose sight of the fear or anxiety that is now coursing through the organisation. This is particularly prevalent in the middle management ranks facing change in almost every facet of their activities. The group should consider regular 'change management workshops' designed to help managers learn how to share information and improve trust.

The work of the group will put considerable pressure on the Human Resources function. There will be other resource implications involved in change which could also cause bottlenecks. The group should be aware of this issue and ensure that outside help is available and applied to assist areas under pressure.

Teamwork

Throughout this week we have emphasised the importance of teamwork. There is a danger as we move into implementation, that the concept of work or multi-disciplinary teams is not properly understood. In this arena, effective teamwork is not just a matter of 'getting on together' or achieving synergy from discussion.

Re-engineering will break down the traditional functional organisation, and redesign the company around processes. Many of these processes will be delivered through multi-disciplinary teams designed to provide customers with a single point of access to meet their needs and wants. In that context, the 'one stop' teams will use technology to share 'specialist' knowledge through 'generalist' workers.

For teams to work effectively in this mode the generalists will need to extend their skills and knowledge. At the same time the specialist has to learn new behaviour patterns and involve themselves with the team. Front line clerical and technical workers have spent several years building a range of skills. They were encouraged along these paths for the benefit of the organisation and their own careers. Skills and skill mixes built up over years are not easily changed overnight.

Education and training

The issues we have just been discussing will underline the importance of education and training for the success of BPR. Throughout the eighties, a variety of quality and redeployment initiatives highlighted the need for more investment in education in industry and commerce. There are signs that executives are learning that the cost of ignorance is greater than the price of education. BPR with its need for re-skilling is helping to accelerate this change in attitude.

The educational syllabus must not only include specific skill training to fit employees for new roles but, also be designed to help change the operating environment. It needs to be closely aligned to the personnel policies being established for BPR. This means that the educational and communication strategies are two sides of the same coin.

Adult learning in business is most effective when it directly relates to the workplace. Employees at all levels are more likely to understand and retain knowledge if they have an easy transition with practice of a new concept and then an immediate opportunity to apply the concepts to their own work.

Business education and training courses have a tendency to create indigestion with the amount of material presented. The most effective method for the business student is to break down the theory into small bites, which can be practised with colleagues in a workshop and then immediately tested in the real environment. Short weekly sessions will prove more effective than concentrated courses.

The educational strategy has broader objectives than training people for BPR. It has to play an essential part in establishing the culture of the organisation. That culture will relate to the vision discussed on Monday, which must be shared with all employees. Education and training should reinforce principles such as open and frank communication. Additionally it should instill an attitude of commitment to continuous improvement in every employee.

Summary

We have spent Friday considering what is required to turn all the preparatory and design work into a successful implementation. In doing that we looked at:

- The implementation plan
- The importance of pilot proofing
- Goals and objectives and the supporting metrics
- The key element of people
- Multi-disciplinary teams and their impact
- Education and training
- The part played by good communication

Holding the gains

On Friday, we examined the factors involved in
implementation. Some of the same factors, and others raised
earlier in the week, will continue to influence the
management of the new organisation. Therefore, to some
extent, Saturday will be a summary chapter of ideas
expressed earlier, though perhaps from another perspective.
The key areas for Saturday can be summarised under the
following headings:

- Recognising the change
- Managing the re-engineered business
- Managing the people dimension
- Maintaining the change
- Exploiting the gains
- Conclusion

Recognising the change

The change resulting from a BPR programme is dramatic, indeed for many traumatic. It changes the very shape of the organisation, it alters relationships both within and without the company and it creates a culture focused on the customer. Yet for too many senior managers the new world comes as a complete surprise. These same managers have sat in on many of the meetings, read the design reports and agreed the recommendations. Vision and reality can be poles apart; many just cannot, or will not, envision what change will mean. If senior management continue with their myopia the management of change will be hindered. The change masters must ensure that there is a high awareness of the day-to-day activities of change. Only then will *all* management recognise and support the new direction.

Some of the changes that they should expect to recognise and react to can be summarised as follows:

- Work units change from functional departments to process-customer-oriented teams
- Employees focus more on their customers, both internal and external, than their bosses
- Employees who once did what they were told now make decisions on their own. They change from controlled to empowered. BPR encourages employees not to just follow rules but to make their own rules

- Jobs change from simple repetitious tasks to multi-dimensional work. This has massive implications for retraining and perhaps more importantly, the future attitudes of those employees. A potential to be released or a destructive force?
- The traditional lines and channels of communication, beloved by many managers, are now obsolete. People communicate with those *they* need to
- Traditionally, managers allocated, supervised, controlled and checked work as it moved from one employee or department to another. These are now team decisions and it is clear that we no longer need all those managers. Will they be able to adapt to the teamwork ethic?
- Team process employees are collectively responsible for process results rather than individually responsible for tasks
- All employees will be paid based on performance (which may be measured on a team basis) rather than status and will be promoted on ability rather than longevity

The author would add one other change in perception in which he appears to be at odds with all the gurus and experts. We are continually being admonished to eliminate all processes which do not add value. In the author's perception, **all** processes add cost not value. Only if all the processes are in balance with market needs do *any* of them add value. That simple perception can take out another layer of subjective influence on decisions.

Managing the re-engineered business

The management goal for BPR and indeed for any improvement initiative should be to enhance the organisation's ability to meet its strategic objectives. In support of that goal, they should be aiming to strengthen, rather than destroy, the organisation's culture.

The level of change, upheaval and confusion must be managed by effective leadership which concentrates on communicating a shared vision for owners, leaders and employees.

In support of that vision, senior management must pay careful attention to the people side of change and at the same time remain focused on measuring and monitoring *process* performance.

Managing the people dimension

Experience has shown that unless an organisation approaches the people dimension in a committed and systematic manner, it will fail. We discussed some of the issues involved on Friday, now we should go a little further into pay and reward.

BPR is changing the way employees work, both collectively and individually. This requires that we re-examine the way we measure employee performance and the way we reward that performance with pay and recognition. An important element of that examination is to focus on the right measures to meet the change from a functional structure to a process driven organisation.

Companies tend to eliminate steadily the annual performance reviews and appraisal systems and to introduce a continuous review system related to team dynamics. The new emphasis on process and team performance provides a much fairer basis for appraisal. Pay may be related to team performance but individuals receive extra payments for learning new skills and specific contributions to the team.

In addition to pay and reward, it is essential to develop and maintain a continuous communications process throughout the organisation. This should be a specific high level responsibility.

Maintaining the change

The re-engineered organisation sets a challenge to managers. It will be demanding but provide high job satisfaction. We are now managing clearly defined processes with specific responsibilities, accountabilities and metrics. Managerial performance is open and measurable.

On the other side of the coin to job satisfaction will come team working and the power to make the decisions about managers' own processes. The manager will decide how best to use the team's capabilities, within company policy, to achieve the objectives, i.e., leadership rather than managing or controlling. Overall, there will be much less reporting up the hierarchical ladder, but more accountability for performance.

We have stressed the importance of measurement before, but this is the real key to maintaining the effectiveness of the changed processes. A process that is not measured and monitored will soon exhibit the signs of neglect and inertia. Performance measures for the key processes are as much the provenance of senior management as for the process manager. If they *are* key processes, they are at the heart of the business performance.

The guidelines for measuring the performance of re-engineered processes are as follows:

- Insist that the designers develop performance measures that would provide an accurate and timely picture of the overall progress of the process *and* the business
- The measures should directly relate to both the business strategy and the process
- All measures should be dynamic so that they reflect the changing conditions of business

- Respond to the measures by changing strategy, goals and the process design where appropriate
- Ensure that the results of all measures are communicated to all the appropriate people

The business readers will have noted the synergy between the concepts of TQM and the methods of BPR. The concept of continuous improvement (the micro level) associated with TQM is now needed to manage the re-engineered process.

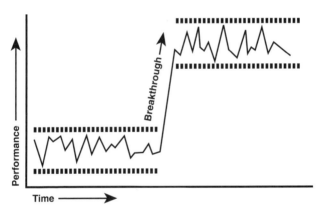

This diagram could reflect the current breakthrough change from a set of processes to the newly re-engineered process. All the attitudes, tools and techniques of TQM can be used to maintain the gain achieved. The diagram may also reflect the future. An attitude of continuous improvement could lead to the next breakthrough.

Exploiting the gains

Everything that we have discussed this week has involved some form of change. Sometimes, managers become so obsessed with the problems created by change that they fail to see the opportunities *presented* by change.

To recognise the possibilities, the manager only needs to consider one element of change, namely, changing relationships. Whatever else happens, the advent of BPR, and all the activities we have described, has irrevocably changed the organisations's relationship with its customers and suppliers. It is also inconceivable that the relationship between management and employees has remained as before. In a mechanistic sense, it is also true that the intricate relationships within the network of business processes has now changed.

Each of those changed relationships has to be managed, but each of them provides an opportunity for developing the business or for finding new targets for BPR. For example, the level of investment and upheaval the organisation has gone through to delight customers can be marketed. Customers have similar problems in their social and business lives. Nowadays, they tend to be intolerant of error, but react very positively to perceived customer orientation.

Philip Crosby, the American quality guru, has a final management step entitled 'Do it all over again'. In a sense we need that attitude in BPR. We started by accepting no boundaries and asking *why* of everything we examined. To exploit the gains **keep asking why**.

Summary

Today we have considered:

- Involving everyone in the change
- Managing the new business
- Understanding the people issues
- Holding the gains

Conclusion

This week we have seen that BPR requires dedication, acceptance of risk and considerable upheaval. Not every organisation is capable of accomplishing the level of change required, but any company that has the ambition to be among the best cannot ignore BPR; indeed they must accept the challenge.

The Business in a Week series

Doing Business in Europe in a Week
Finance for Non-Financial Managers in a Week
Introduction to Bookkeeping and Accounting in a Week
Succeeding at Interviews in a Week
Successful Appraisals in a Week
Successful Assertiveness in a Week
Successful Budgeting in a Week
Successful Business Writing in a Week
Successful Career Planning in a Week
Successful Computing for Business in a Week
Successful Customer Care in a Week
Successful Direct Mail in a Week
Successful Interviewing in a Week
Successful Leadership in a Week
Successful Market Research in a Week
Successful Marketing in a Week
Successful Meetings in a Week
Successful Mentoring in a Week
Successful Motivation in a Week
Successful Negotiating in a Week
Successful Presentation in a Week
Successful Project Management in a Week
Successful Purchasing in a Week
Successful Selling in a Week
Successful Stress Management in a Week
Successful Time Management in a Week
Successful Training in a Week
Understanding BPR in a Week
Understanding Just in Time in a Week
Understanding Quality Management Standards in a Week
Understanding Total Quality Management in a Week
Understanding VAT in a Week